MICKY B's DIARY

My Endless Quest to Find a Friend

Nanny Bernie
aka
Bernice Bose

ARTHUR H. STOCKWELL LTD
Torrs Park, Ilfracombe, Devon, EX34 8BA
Established 1898
www.ahstockwell.co.uk

© *Bernice Bose, 2019*
First published in Great Britain, 2019

The moral rights of the author have been asserted.

All rights reserved.
No part of this publication may be reproduced
or transmitted in any form or by any means,
electronic or mechanical, including photocopy,
recording, or any information storage and
retrieval system, without permission
in writing from the copyright holder.

British Library Cataloguing-in-Publication Data.
A catalogue record for this book is available
from the British Library.

DEDICATION

To Micky and Joey, for all the pleasure they've given to myself and my family.

ISBN 978-0-7223-4945-8
Printed in Great Britain by
Arthur H. Stockwell Ltd
Torrs Park   Ilfracombe
Devon EX34 8BA

ABOUT THE AUTHOR

I was born at a very early age in West Ewell, Surrey. I remember, for some strange reason, being very scared of dogs – so much so that when my parents asked me to post a letter in the postbox 300 yards away, at the end of our road, I would make a detour to avoid a little dog that ran down the side of its house to bark at passers-by. It was only doing its job!

However, many years later I became very fond of my three daughters' dogs and cats. I first started writing a 'dog diary' about Micky and Joey some six years ago.

My daughters and grandchildren read it and urged me to get it published. So here I am.

Bernice Bose

MICKY B's DIARY
(My Endless Quest to Find a Friend)

SUITABLE FOR DOGS WITH A READING AGE OF 1+

Hello. I am a Bichon Frise called Micky. My human mum and dad are Mark and Jo. This is my story.

A few human years ago, Mum had a beautiful Bichon called Holly. Unfortunately Holly became very unwell and went to doggy heaven. Mum was very upset and sad. However, to cheer her up, someone kind went to the Bichon Frise Rescue Centre. So here the story starts.

7 APRIL 2013

Well, here I am all alone at the Bichon Frise Rescue Centre; my siblings have been chosen and gone to their new homes. I feel so lonely. Mind you, the humans that collected them kept talking about breeding and Crufts – whatever that is. Perhaps it's a doggy disease. Oh well, I'll have a sleep – long time 'til supper.

Hello! There's a lovely young lady and a gentleman with their little boy and girl. They're all looking at me and smiling. Oh! Have all my wishes come true? All I want is a nice mum and dad who love me and a comfy home.

They're taking me home. Never mind supper – let's go!

Lots of tail-wagging now – so happy.

We arrive. Their human kennel is very large and comfy-looking. There are other four-legged creatures here. I think they are cats, and because I'm a dog I'm supposed to chase them. I'm not sure what to do, so I'll ignore them. Now we're off again, around a giant puddle that the humans call a pond. There are lots of two-legged animals here with strange feet. I try to chase them, but they do a lot of flapping and go up in the sky.

    Then we arrive at Jo's house (my new mum). Her eyes start leaking and she gives me a big cuddle. Yes, my dreams have all come true. I like my new mum and I'm going to be so happy living here with her in her big human kennel.

8 APRIL 2013

In the morning Mum goes to work at the human vet's to earn money to feed me, so I have to go in a big cage. It's very roomy and comfortable and I've got all my toys to play with and a bowl of water. After a while Mum comes back home and feeds me, then she gives me a lovely cuddle and takes me for a walk around the big puddle. I ignore the big white two-legged things. Don't want to play with them anyway. Then it's back home and in my cage again until Mum comes back later.

    Mum's home – more cuddles and food and we go for another walk around the puddle.

    Later we go to bed. Mum's bed is very comfortable. I hope I can sleep here when Dad comes home. I don't think he'll fit in my cage!

12 APRIL 2013

When Mum comes home from the human vet's we go off to stay at Nanny B's and John's. It's a long, boring journey so I have a good sleep in my travel cage.

    When Mum parks the car she puts me in my dog-carrying bag (not to be confused with a doggy bag)!

    Nan and John are nice and there are lots of new things to sniff at and places to explore. And so to bed. . . .

13 APRIL 2013

Off we go to Epsom and the Doll's House shop. It's not open yet so we go across the road for a coffee. I'm hiding in my dog bag (again not to be confused with a doggy bag)! Suddenly there's a bit of a commotion. Mum has thrown a cup of coffee over Nan! I don't think she meant to.

The Doll's House man is very nice; Mum and Nan spend lots of money! Now we're off to see Mark, Angela and Joseph. Angela is one of mum's sisters – my aunty.

Joseph is a bit wary of me. I only want to play with his toes.

This morning I learnt to climb the stairs at Nan's, and here at Aunty Angela's the stairs are in the big room. I had a great time running up them!

Uncle Mark and Joseph had not a good time bringing me back down again.

Then back to Nan's for tea.

After tea I went exploring. There are lots of new smells to sniff.

All of a sudden I felt very strange. My legs wouldn't work very well and I couldn't see properly, so I kept bumping into things. I started crying because I was very scared. Mum thought my tummy was hurting cos I'd swallowed one of her false fingernails, but I think I must have eaten something that I found on the floor.

14 APRIL 2013

Mum is crying and she and Nan have taken me to the vet's.

I had to stay at the vet's all night and Mum and Nan picked me up this morning. I am fine now, thank goodness. Mum and Nan were very worried.

Off we go back home. Granddad is coming to stay.

21 APRIL 2013

Had a nice week with Granddad. Think I stressed him out a bit cos I was naughty – but hey, that's what puppies do! Mum's neighbour pops in and lets me out in the garden for a run and play. She's very nice. Dad's coming home. Hope he's OK. Up to now I've only had Mum to annoy. Yes, Dad's fine and he's been paying me a lot of attention. I like it. He refuses to sleep in my cage, but I'm allowed on the bed.

MAY 2013

Dad's away again, but not for long. In the meantime I've made friends with Bumble next door. We talk to each other through the fence, which is a bit boring; so I tried to dig under the fence, but Mum stopped me. She put a big hairy thing on a pole in the way of my tunnel, but Bumble attacked it. He's my hero! I've made a few friends at the giant pond. The strange-looking things with funny big yellow feet – they like bread! Then I got bored so I bit Mum's feet. She didn't find it very funny.

Same old dog days. Lots of walks, cuddles and being a bit naughty and getting told off. Then Mum starts laughing, so everything is OK.

I'm allowed out of my cage! Dad has made me my own door to get out into the garden, so I can go and explore when Mum's working at the human vet's.
    Found a lovely white four-legged friend in the garden. I

tried to follow her through the fence then found out she was a cat! So not a friend.

Same old, same old. Nothing much happening, but very relaxing. I keep reflecting (as dogs usually don't do) and thinking what it was like in my previous home at the Bichon Frise Rescue Centre.

The human carers there were lovely, and all of them were very nice and gave us all the care and attention we needed. But I'm so glad that I'm here with my new human mum and dad. They are both so kind and loving. The young lady, gentleman and little boy and girl who picked me from the rescue centre come to Mum's and see me a lot. They are all very kind and gentle. I am such a lucky Bichon.

It's Cousin Emma's birthday. We're going to visit tomorrow and also see John and Nanny Bernie – or Nanny B for short. I must avoid the drugs on the floor this time. Whoopee, Dad's home! He's ignoring me cos Mum wants the lights wired up!

BBQ at Aunty Debbie's. I was looking forward to meeting Cousin Frankie (yellow Lab), but he wasn't very friendly. Uncle Dennis said that it was because Frankie was out for a walk when I arrived and he thought that I was intruding on his territory. Lots of lovely food for the humans, but not for me, although I manage to encounter a dropped sausage now and then!

Been having a lovely time. I go to puppy training. It's great fun, but I don't think that it's supposed to be. Lots of other puppies to play with.

Up to stay with Nanny B and John. Mum and Nan went out, so I had to amuse John by running off with bits of tissue and doing other naughty things.

Nanny B is here. Mum has got an interview in Poole in Dorset at a large human vet's. We are now going to be living in Dorset. I was the last to know, but I'm only a dog! Mum wants to get a job before we move there. Mum got the job, so I think we're moving.

JUNE 2013

The family are all down. They all went to a christening. When they got back they were all giggling and kept mentioning Muriel's organ playing!

Mum and Dad are at home for a few weeks. Having a brilliant time. Visited lots of places, including a lovely little house in Dorset. I think it's going to be my new home.

JULY TO SEPTEMBER 2013

I think there are things going on. Lots of boxes everywhere! I've been so busy nosing in the boxes and other dog-forbidden areas that I haven't had time to write my diary. I've remembered a few things though.

19 OCTOBER 2013

It's Cousin James's twenty-first birthday party. Frankie, the yellow Lab, just doesn't like me. I don't know why. When I went to see him in the kitchen to play he growled at me so I cocked my leg on a kitchen cabinet! I don't think anyone saw me! Had a great time. Even spotted a few titbits dropped on the floor! Took Nanny B back home and then we went home.

20 OCTOBER 2013

Mum made a nice-smelling dinner, but I wasn't allowed any. Nanny Ann came round. She fell asleep after dinner, but then made a funny noise which woke her up. She tried to blame me! It wasn't me! Mum and Dad were laughing.

24 OCTOBER 2013

Nanny B is here! Goody, goody – someone else to annoy. Mum took me to the groomer's today. I enjoyed it. I felt good cos my puppy fluff had almost gone.

Jo (the groomer's Bichon) won't play with me. He's posh and snooty. Mum said that because he has bouffant fur he looks like a big girl's blouse. Never seen one, so I don't know what she meant. Mum and Nanny B went out, then Dad came home. Ashley and Sophie, Bonnie and Beau came round (they got me from the Bichon Frise Rescue Centre for Mum). They all had a lovely dinner, but I had dry biscuits again. It's not fair.

25 OCTOBER 2013

All up early. Then Mum, Dad and Nanny B went off in the car and left me alone. Sophie, Beau and Bonnie came to see me. Then I was on my own again.

Suddenly Mum, Dad and Nanny B came home in a huge white van. Perhaps we're going on a big round-the-world adventure.

NO, WE'RE MOVING TO OUR NEW HOUSE IN DORSET IN NOVEMBER.

They loaded up nearly all our furniture into the van. Then we all went to bed. I tried to get into Nan's room, but she ignored my cries. I'll get her in the morning!

26 OCTOBER 2013

Nan had to go home cos there was going to be a storm and she was worried.

Mum took me for a nice long walk, then we all got into the

big white van and set off. After a very long time we arrived at a pretty-big human kennel. Mum told me it was my new home. There's a place out the back with a special play pit for me. Also there's a green hopping thing, which hopped off and hid somewhere. Thought that I'd have someone to play with at last, but no. We then drove back to our old house; we arrived there late and all went to bed. I'm so excited!

5 NOVEMBER 2013

We've now moved into our new home. Every morning we take Dad to work and then Mum takes me for a long walk. There are lots of stones and a giant puddle and you can't see where it ends. The puddle keeps moving, and when it does the stones move as well and make a strange noise. Suddenly a giant bird with whirring wings on its head appears. Mum says it's a helicopter, not a bird. That's a relief. I wouldn't stand a chance if that swooped down and got me. Mum waved at one of them. I will tell Dad tonight – she's mad. Mum's not working at the moment, so we go for lovely long walks. Sometimes we see quite big white things with four legs and they come over to the fence and say, "Hello." I thought that they might be my cousins or family, but Mum said they're sheep. I shall call them my friends.

28 NOVEMBER 2013

Nan's here. Whoopee! She can come with us on our long walks and I can show her my sheep friends. Aunty Eileen (Nan's sister, who lives nearby) dropped her off.

29 NOVEMBER 2013

Mum dropped Dad off at work. Then we went for a long walk along Chesil Beach. This is where the big puddle starts. Mum and Nan then went shopping. They seemed very excited when they got back. We've been invaded by humans. In the evening Aunty Eileen came to see us with Tricia (Nan's niece) and her man friend. Mum cooked something delicious for them. Me? Dry biscuits again. Then they all went to bingo – whatever that is.

30 NOVEMBER 2013

Two men humans delivered a big white cupboard and Mum put food in it. Then we went for a long walk, watched television and went to bed.

1 DECEMBER 2013

Nan's going home. Mum is upset.

2 DECEMBER 2013

Been for a long walk with Mum. Ate a dead bird and it made me sick. Mum said it was my fault and told me off. Then she gave me a cuddle.

24 DECEMBER 2013

Mum, Dad and me went to Nanny Ann's to stay. Nanny Ann kept telling me off. She wouldn't let me dig a tunnel under her fence. I only wanted to meet a new friend. He kept talking to me through the fence. However, he sounds very big, so perhaps I won't make him my friend.

25 DECEMBER 2013

We all went to my old human kennel, where Ashley, Sophie, Bonnie and Beau now live. They've got cats, but they don't like me. Lots of presents – even for me.

26 DECEMBER 2013

Off to see Granddad. Then down to Nanny B's and John's. Nan and John are nice, but they didn't feed me. I had to eat some grass. Mum and Dad came home and we went back to our new kennel in Dorset. Where we live now is called Piddlehinton!

27–31 DECEMBER 2013

Dad and Mum are both off work. Great fun! This morning I escaped and ran off to see my sheep friends. Dad chased me and Mum played with me, enticing me back with treats. But I haven't seen my sheep friends for ages and they're the only friends I've got. It was very funny – Mum still had her pyjamas on!

1 JANUARY 2014

Mum has a new friend that she met this morning when we went out for our walk. Mum's friend has got a big dog who likes me! His dangly bits are the same height as my nose.

8 JANUARY 2014

It's Mum's birthday. She cried when she opened my card. Then she and Dad laughed. I gave her some money as I thought it would be handy (actually Dad put it in the card). Mum goes to work now so I'm by myself. But we go for a nice walk in the morning and in the evening. Later on I sit on the window sill upstairs so that I can see Mum and Dad park the car outside.

9–18 JANUARY 2014

We still go out for walks if it's not too cold or wet. I haven't seen my sheep friends for ages. Perhaps they don't like the wet, cold weather and the dark.

Mum said that Aunty Angela, Uncle Mark and Joseph are coming to see us soon.

19–24 JANUARY 2014

Mum's got some boots to wear for when we go out for walks. She looks like a farmer.

25 JANUARY 2014

Mum took me to a new groomer in town at a big pet shop. I had a haircut and Mum said that I looked very handsome, so she took photos of me.

I peed up the bags of cat litter on the way through to the groomer's.

26 JANUARY 2014

Aunty Angela, Uncle Mark and Cousin Joseph are here. Whoopee, more people to annoy! They've brought some stuff from Nan. I think it's some of her clothes. Oh heck, she's not going to move in with us, is she? No, it's for when she comes to stay. Aunty Angela said that there's something in the Mary Poppins bag for Mum and Dad and something for me, but I'm not allowed it yet. Wonder if I can get my nose in the bag when they're not looking? Best not. Nan's undies might be in there – YUK!

27 JANUARY 2014

Aunty Angela, Uncle Mark and Cousin Joseph are going home. Mum is crying. We've all had good fun.

28 JANUARY 2014

It's been very cold and wet and windy. Now Mum is working too we go for early walks and it's very dark and cold, but good fun. Then Mum and Dad go to work and I'm all warm and cosy indoors. When they get home I am so excited to see them.

They give me a treat for being good and a nice cuddle and we go for a quick walk in the dark. I haven't seen my sheep friends for a long time.

31 JANUARY 2014

It's my birthday! I am one year old. Nan has sent me a lovely card and some money for treats or a bone.

7 FEBRUARY 2014

Nanny Ann and Uncle Rob have come to stay. We've had a great time.

8–21 FEBRUARY 2014

Nothing happening. It's so cold and dark, but we've still been on some nice walks. We have a lovely fire made with wood and coal. It's very cosy. I ate some coal that was in a bucket. It tasted quite nice!

22 FEBRUARY 2014

Aunty Angela, Uncle Mark and Joseph are here. Great fun! Mum has got a nice new bedcover with shiny buttons on it – very tempting.
I've given in to temptation: one button off the cover. I've hidden it under Mum's bed. Hope she doesn't see it. I'll be in trouble.

23 FEBRUARY 2014

Everyone's gone home. I'm bored. Even the green hopping thing in the garden has disappeared. The lady next door said that it is very rare and is protected. It seems even rarer now. When will I ever find a friend?
Think I'll go and chew another button off the cover.

24 FEBRUARY TO 4 MARCH 2014

Lots of early morning walks and in the dark in the evenings. Cold and wet and dark. Lots of play and cuddles, but very boring.
I can't chew any more buttons off the cover. Mum found them under the bed and I got told off. She's tried to fold the cover up to hide the buttons, but I was watching her! Best leave them alone.

5 MARCH 2014

Nanny B is here! Went for a walk with Mum and Nan.

Watched television then we all went to bed.

I went to sleep on Nan's bed, but she kept me awake making noises with her nose.

6 MARCH 2014

Up early and out for a walk with Mum. Then Mum and Dad went to work.

Nan did something to the fire, then she started doing something to Mum's clothes with a hissing thing. Suddenly she said a rude word. One of Mum's clothes has got a hole in it! She'll be in trouble. At least it's not my fault.

I bit her toes twice! I don't think she liked it, cos she told me off.

Then the person came who puts things through the hole in the door for me to play with. She wouldn't let me have them. Then Nan got the push-around thing out that sucks up things off the floor. I ran upstairs and hid . . . just in case.

Had a nice sleep on Nan's bed. When I came downstairs Nan was sitting on the seat in front of the window, so I climbed up and sat on the window sill and pretended to look out of the window watching for Mum and Dad to come home.

Got bored so I attacked Nan's head. I did it very gently in case it fell off, cos she's very old. I don't think she liked it much, cos she called me a rude name.

7 MARCH 2014

Mum and Dad are taking Nan home. It's a long journey and I have to sit in the back with Nan and wear my harness. Nan has one too. Perhaps it's cos she's so old.

It's horrid and I can't move much, but I'll try. Oh dear! I've been fidgeting and now the harness is twisted and strangling me. Dad has to stop the car and untangle me. Whoopee! I'm free and sitting on Nan's lap. She opened the window so that I can put my head out, but Dad told her that I would jump out, so she shut it quickly and nearly took my head off!

We arrived at Nan's house and then Mum and Dad disappeared. They came back, but then they took Nan out and left me with Johnny. I had to amuse him by ripping up bits of tissue paper, though I don't think he found it that funny.

We're off again to Aunty Debbie's. Frankie is there, but I'm keeping near Mum.

8 MARCH 2014

We stayed at Granddad's and then we went to Nan's again. Mum is stealing Nan's car! No, she's not! Nan has got a new car. She's given her old one to Dad.

9 MARCH 2014

Dad has put a roundabout up in the garden, but I can't get on it cos it's too high. Anyway, Mum is putting her clothes on it and they're having a great time going around and around in circles.

Dad has made a hole in the back door. I can get through it and get out into the garden. Not sure if I'm allowed, so I only go through it when Mum and Dad are out.

10 MARCH 2014

Mother's Day. Don't know what that means, and the only mother I know is Jo.

We're staying at Nanny Ann's house. She took me for a nice walk while Mum and Dad went out. Nanny B and Aunty Angela came and then we all went home.

11–31 MARCH 2014

It's not wet or muddy any more and it's warmer. Still haven't seen my little white friends.

APRIL 2014

Not much going on, so nothing to write about in my diary.
People have been coming to stay.

MAY 2014

It was Nan's birthday on 1 May. Everyone there – good fun!
Nan bought me a ham bone and a sausage roll (doggy ones), but there were lots of other things around so I saved them for later.

3 JUNE 2014

Mum took me to the dog hospital. Had a sharp thing put in me. It hurt and I went to sleep. When I woke up I felt a bit strange. I have a feeling something's missing. Mum and Dad collected me and took me home.
Mum's got new earrings! They're round and dangly!

JULY TO SEPTEMBER 2014

It's been a very busy time. Lots of humans staying, so lots of fun, but haven't had time to write it all in my diary.
I had a little brown four-legged friend come and visit me to play. We played chase. It was good fun. He moved about very quickly. I didn't get a chance to catch him. All of a sudden he ran behind Mum's vegetable box, so I chased him and the box fell over. Then he ran back out into the garden. There were

vegetables all over the floor. I suppose I'll get the blame – better go upstairs and hide.

Dad saw him that evening and murdered him accidentally. Another friend gone.

OCTOBER 2014

Dad's got the big box with wheels on out of the secret room in the roof. Mum is putting clothes in it. I know what that means: abandoned again. I don't mind though cos I'm going to the Dog Holiday Camp. Mum took me to see it two days ago and it looks good. Perhaps I'll make a friend there as long as Dad doesn't get in there.

NOVEMBER 2014

Something's happening. Mum has put two trees in the house with lights and dangly things on. Looks like fun. Whoops! There goes a snowman and an angel. The angel was ugly anyway. She was cross-eyed.

DECEMBER 2014

Yes, something is happening. I think it's called Christmas. Lots of lights everywhere and things hanging from the ceiling. Too high for me to reach. There's a new angel on one of the trees. She's quite pretty, but it looks like she's not got underwear on!

Lots of humans staying.

JANUARY 2015

House looks empty now that the trees and lights and the humans have gone.

31 January is my birthday! I'm two years old. Can't have a party, cos I haven't got any friends – thanks to Dad! I wonder if he had anything to do with my sheep friends disappearing.

I got some nice cards with pictures of dogs on and lots of treats and bone money.

We went to the seaside. (It's not a giant pond.) We had a lovely day. Uncle Rob, Aunty Dionne, Nanny Ann, Little Rob and Reggie came to stay.

FEBRUARY 2015

The young lady at the groomer's in the big pet shop is learning about dogs and she wants me to be her project. I'm going to be a model! I wish I hadn't cocked my leg on the big bags of cat litter when we came in. Hope she didn't see me.

Aunty Angela, Uncle Mark and Joseph are staying.

MARCH 2015

Nanny B, Aunty Angela, Uncle Mark and Joseph are still staying. I think they like it here in Piddlehinton! We all went to Moreton. A famous man is buried there in the churchyard (T. E. Lawrence). The humans all went to find his grave. I peed on it!

We all went to a nice food place. I had nothing. I had a drink of water from a smelly puddle. Then we all went for a walk and I had a swim in a big puddle.

Then we all went home.

When we all got home they all had dinner and I had a lovely bone to chew.

I wasn't very well in the night. I think the bone upset my tummy, or it could have been the smelly water I drank.

Something has occurred in the downstairs loo! It wasn't me.

Next day everyone went home. Nanny B and Mum were crying.

I feel better today although my bottom is still a bit itchy!

Me and Joey swimming in the pool at Moreton, where I got told off for peeing on T. E. Lawrence's grave, March 2015.

APRIL TO DECEMBER 2015

No entries in diary. Too busy!

MAY 2016

Oh no! The big box on wheels is out again. This time Mum and Nanny B are going somewhere. That's all right – I'll still have Dad to annoy.

[Two weeks later] Mum and Nanny B are back. They are both wearing silly hats and T-shirts with 'PELVIS' written on them. A bit personal if you ask me.

JUNE 2016

Oh, I am so happy! I've got a new friend. A forever one. His name is Joey.

Dad felt sorry for me cos he thought I was lonely, so he went to the Bichon Frise Rescue Centre and chose Joey. He is sixteen months old, so old enough to go out for walks and for me to play with. His birthday is 1 February – the day after mine. We can have a party next year. He's very friendly, but he barks a lot. Mum says it's because he wants attention. Can you buy dog earplugs? A friend at last! My seemingly endless task to find a friend is finally over.

Mum takes us both out for walks. It's still wet everywhere and we get a bit muddy, so we both get scrubbed with our special shampoo when we get in. Nanny B used it by mistake once! I thought her head fur looked a bit strange!

JULY 2016

It's been so hot we haven't been out for long walks. I think we'll both be going to the groomer's soon. I'll show Joey where to cock his leg when we get there.

5 AUGUST 2016

Whoopee! Nanny B, Aunty Angela and Joseph are here. Mum has gone to work at the human vet's. We've had a great time.

6 AUGUST 2016

Dad's gone to work. Mum, Nan, Aunty Angela and Joseph are going out. We're not. We're going to stick our nose under the back gate and cry. Until they've gone!

Everyone is back home now. We've had a nice walk. Aunty Angela's head fur is very thick. I can't wait to attack it.

7 AUGUST 2016

Nanny B is doing something in the garden. She's putting things in the play pit. We're not allowed to dig in it any more. Joey and me have buried some nice tasty morsels there, and when Nan finds them she throws them away. Dad is making lunch and cooking something exciting for dinner tonight. Not for us though.

8 AUGUST 2016

Nan, Aunty Angela and Joseph are going home. It always makes Mum cry.

SEPTEMBER 2016

Uncle Dennis and Aunty Debbie are here. Uncle Dennis has got something on his arm. It looks a bit like our harnesses, but in the wrong place. We'll wait and see if Aunty Debbie takes him out for a walk.

OCTOBER 2016

Boxes on wheels are out. Abandoned again. Both parents have gone. We are orphans! We don't mind really – we will have a good time at the dog hotel.

I suppose we'll be put up for adoption. Well, we shall bite the humans if we don't like the look of them. Oh well, no one has turned up to look at us and we're having a good time catching up with our old friends here. We can only wait and see what happens.

Mum and Dad are back. They've gone a funny colour. Mum is crying – perhaps she's missed us. Well, we're not giving in. We will bark and sulk forever and be naughty.

We can't sulk any more as it's upsetting Mum. But how would they feel if Joey and me just took off like they did? Lots of cuddles from Mum, and Dad just laughs.

I'll get him later. He won't be able to find his socks for ages.

5 NOVEMBER 2016

It's Bonfire Night. Last week it was Halloween. Don't know what they mean, but Mum and Dad put two large, round orange things in the window with candles in them.

Will check Dad out next time he comes out of the shower. Lots of loud bangs and flashes outside.

12 NOVEMBER 2016

Oh no! Bags are out. It's OK – dog bowls being packed – we're off!

Arrive at Nanny Ann's. Mum has brought a big pot with her and we think there's something yummy in it. We won't get any though. All we get is boring dog stuff.

Now Nanny B, Angela and Joseph are here. Nanny B has got something doggy in her bag. I tried to get it, but I can't. At last Nan has got our treats out: two doggy bagels.

I know there's something else in her bag. Yes, we're allowed them.

Ashley and Sophie are here with their two little humans. They're very sweet.

Now everyone's going. Never mind – it's been a lovely day.

3–4 DECEMBER 2016

Lots of things going on now. Loads of lights everywhere. Santa has been mentioned. Apparently he comes down the chimney and delivers presents. Hope not. He'll burn his bum. He probably only brings presents for humans anyway. There's also a tree, but we're not allowed to pee up it. What else are trees for? Wow! Frankie's parents are here.

Dad and Uncle Dennis are watching a game on the television. We think it's called football. Lots of men humans running about on the grass kicking a ball. When they get the ball in a net they almost cry, then they hug each other and lift their shirts up! Strange!

Mum and Aunty Debbie have taken me and Joey for a nice walk. We're all hungry now. Mum has cooked something yummy. Not for us though.

10 DECEMBER 2016

Mum's putting her coat on. Alone again? No, Dad's staying here. We can play him up.

Mum's back. She's been to meet up with her family in a faraway place. She's been eating something nice – Chinese, I think. I can smell it.

22 DECEMBER 2016

Lots more going on now. All kinds of lovely food being put into the big, cold cupboard. It's for Christmas. This seems to happen every year. Still don't know what it means. Again, like last year, there's a tree in the room and we're told again not to pee up it. It's very tempting though. Oh, here's Aunty Angela, Uncle Mark and Joseph. Who can we annoy first? Lots of nice dinners they're eating, but not us.

As usual we get the boring dog stuff.

23–24 DECEMBER 2016

Still lots going on. The humans have all gone mad. Wish they'd all go upstairs to sleep. They're getting on our nerves. Thank dogness they've all gone out. We keep searching, but can't find anything naughty to do.

Now they're all back home and all being silly. We tried to annoy Granddad, but he just ignored us.

At last – off to bed.

25 DECEMBER 2016

They're all still fast asleep. We want food and a nice walk. They're up again and eating more food. Now we're going for a nice walk. Back in the big human kennel they're having drinks and they've got lots of stuff wrapped in paper. We've got some too. Then later, after another walk, they're eating again. Mum has made a beautiful dinner. All the humans are eating it and saying how delicious it is.

We are allowed a few skinny sausages. Mum calls them pigs in blankets. Don't think I'll have one now. On second thoughts, I'll bury it for later.

We don't know much about this Christmas thing, but it seems that it's a time in the year for humans to go mad – or even madder in this house! We're glad we are dogs. Everyone's watching the television now. There's a human on it called Paul O'Grady. He's at a place that looks like a dogs' Butlin's, but our friends don't look very well. Better off here. Mum is crying.

26 DECEMBER 2016

Everyone's gone home now and we're on our own with Dad. Mum's gone to the human vet's to get money to feed us.

31 DECEMBER 2016

Something else is occurring now. Humans are behaving in a strange way.

Lots of explosions. Can't be Mum's or Dad's, because they are followed by pretty colours not bad smells. Mum and Dad are going out to the human food place.

Mum said that it's New Year's Eve. Why does Eve want new ears? Is there something wrong with her old ones?

Mum and Dad back at 1 p.m. They're nuts. But me and Joey love them.

1 JANUARY 2017

Apparently Eve has got her new ears and must be pleased with them cos it's New Ears Day. Mum and Dad look funny. I think they had a bit of a do last night for Eve's new ears. Anyway, a peaceful day with lots of walks in the fresh air and lots of treats. We think Mum and Dad feel guilty cos we haven't had many walks.

8 JANUARY 2017

It's Mum's bath day. Oh crikey! Hope we don't have to get in the bath with her, cos we won't have any treats and the stuff in the bath stings our eyes.

We are alone again. Mum and Dad are meeting up with the other human families. They are going to a place not far away for Chinese. They're soon back home and we have a nice walk.

FEBRUARY 2017

Mum is taking us to Nanny B's and John's. That will be good. John makes a big fuss of us and so does Nan.

We have a lovely week. Lots of nice walks and we visit Aunty Angela, Uncle Mark and Cousin Joseph. Aunty Debbie comes to see us at Aunty Angela's. We went for a nice long walk. Then we went back and went home to Piddlehinton.

MARCH 2017

Back home now and more things happening. Mum and Dad are packing things up in boxes. Hope they're not leaving us. No!

Dad has come home in a giant white car. I think it's called a van. Like the one we used before when we moved to Piddlehinton. Are we going somewhere different? Everything is being loaded into the van.

Me and Joey with Nanny B, 2017.

Me, Joey and Uncle Mark, 2017.

Me and Joey with Mum and Aunty Angela, 2017.

3 MARCH 2017

Yes, we will be leaving Piddlehinton and going to live at Nanny Ann's at Amberstone. Not sure when, but lots of things are happening. When we go to Nanny Ann's Dad puts our entire house upstairs into a dark secret room.

Hope me and Joey haven't got to live there.

5 MARCH 2017

Lots of humans visiting at Nanny Ann's. It's little Bonnie's birthday.

What a lovely day!

6 MARCH 2017

Now we're all back at home in Piddlehinton. Dad has gone to work. Mum is putting lots of things in boxes. Hope me and Joey aren't going in one.

7 MARCH 2017

All back to normal – sort of. Me and Joey sleeping and playing all day.

AUGUST 2017

So much has happened. I've been too busy to write my diary.

We have all moved from Piddlehinton to Amberstone, where Nanny Ann lives. Mum is going to keep Nanny Ann company. Dad will be here at weekends. We see a lot of Bonnie and Beau and all our human family – aunties, uncles and cousins. It's good fun.

Mum has been attacking the dirt in the garden. She makes holes in the dirt, then puts things in the holes. Perhaps we can help. We like digging holes! No, not allowed.

The other week Mum and Dad put a little greenhouse in the garden. It looks like a large kennel. Should be fun for us. Mum's been putting things in the little greenhouse and we're not allowed in there.

Mum has also been doing something strange. She keeps making holes in the humans' food bowls. Then she puts them together, takes them to a crafty place and sells them. She says that people put cakes on them before they eat them.

Sometimes we all go to a big field and the humans put up funny kennels that we all sleep in for a few nights. Last time, Nanny B, Aunty Angela and Joseph came.

All the humans helped each other putting the kennels together. Mum's friend Pam came with her two children, Peter and Annabel. They are nice. They've got two dogs – a friend each for Joey and me? No. But they are friendly and we have good fun playing together. Mum was walking around with a bright-yellow sort of jacket on and a light on her head! I think she must have ASD (attention seeking disorder), cos no one laughed. They just ignored her. Aunty Angela and Nan went home and left Joseph behind. Perhaps he's been naughty and it's his punishment.

NOVEMBER 2017

All the nice sunny days have gone now. Everywhere is chilly and damp.

Me and Joey have had some good times though. Lots of visitors and fun.

I remember one day when it was sunny. Nanny Ann and Mum were having a fight in the garden with the big roundabout – the one they put their clothes on. The roundabout won, but they had a return match a few days later. Nanny Ann and Mum won this time. Then, the next time Mum put some clothes on it, it fell over! They must have knocked it out!

Me and Joey and Mum went to stay at Nanny Bernie's. We had a great time annoying John. He has two nice ladies come and visit, and they help him into bed.

4 NOVEMBER 2017

We went to Aunty Angela's. All our human family was there. It was good fun.

We all went for a walk and there were lots of loud noises. I think Nanny Bernie has a problem – she can't blame that on us!

12 NOVEMBER 2017

Nanny Bernie is here at Amberstone. Whoopee! Lots of treats. She's brought a big black bag with her. We hope that it's full of doggy treats for us. No. Dad has put it in the dark human cupboard upstairs, where we can't get it.

Anyway, we've been for some nice long walks, but haven't seen any sheep friends yet. I wanted to introduce them to Joey. He would love them.

We like Nanny Bernie – she always tickles our tummies and cuddles us. She has brought with her a nice little, unusual green tree. Me and Joey cocked our legs up it – well, that's what trees are for, aren't they?

Nanny Bernie has gone home now. Me and Joey like her a lot, not just because she brings us treats.

25 DECEMBER 2017

It's the beginning of that mad human time of year again. We are all going to Aunty Debbie's and Uncle Dennis's again. Sadly, Frankie is not there.

There are lots of things wrapped in brightly coloured paper

for everyone, and Joey and me have a ripping time!

31 DECEMBER 2017

There are lots of loud exploding things whizzing about in the sky. It's new ears for Eve again.

JOEY AND ME WILL BE STARTING A NEW DIARY FOR 2018.

1 JANUARY 2018

It's New Ears Day AGAIN! Eve gets new ears every year. We get nothing. I suppose it's cos she's a girl.

2–5 JANUARY 2018

It has been very wet and windy, outside *and* indoors!
 Hello! Mum is putting her clothes in cases. Don't know where she's going, but Nanny Bernie is here and they've both driven off somewhere. Abandoned again!
 Never mind. Dad and Nanny Ann are here, so we can annoy them instead.

8 JANUARY 2018

It's Mum's birthday. Where is she? I bought her a special present from the Dog Pound Shop and she's not here. Oh, there she is, just getting out of Nanny Bernie's car. She's brought all her clothes back too. Me and Joey are pleased to see her, but we'll sulk and ignore her for a while. No, she's brought us a present each so we won't sulk too much.
 There are lots of presents for Mum and a nice cake. We're

not allowed cake cos it's bad for dogs – well, apart from Joey. He eats everything and anything. Last Christmas Joey ate a box of Dad's chocolate shells. He was crying with joy!

Joey was OK, but Dad wasn't! Dad was very cross and worried, and we both got told off. Joey went and hid behind the sofa.

Joey hiding cos he ate Dad's chocolate shells, January 2018.

FEBRUARY 2018

All of January and February have been boring – dark, cold and wet. Mum still takes us out for walks and we get very muddy. Then we have to be cleaned outside. Mum uses a green plastic snake that sprays water all over us. It's not very nice, but then Mum takes us indoors and dries us with nice warm towels. We are lucky dogs really and we get a treat.

February is the same as January – cold, dark and wet. It was my birthday on 31 January and Joey's on 1 February, but everyone forgot. Oh no – Nanny Bernie sent us a nice card each and some treat money. But no party for us!

One day, though, Mum took me and Joey and Nanny Ann to Surrey. Nanny Ann wanted to go and see the places where she used to live and work. On the way we collected Aunty Angela and Nanny Bernie. We drove around for a while, and then we went to the human groomer's where Nanny Bernie is groomed. It was where Nanny Ann used to work when she was a young girl. The human groomer there is very nice and she has two little pugs. We are allowed in and we have a great time chasing up and down the shop with Dinky and Tinsel.

Then we dropped Nanny Bernie and Aunty Angela off home and went back to our house.

It was a lovely day and we all had a good time!

MARCH 2018

Lots of visitors – great fun! First of all it was Mother's Day. We don't know where our dog mother is, but we bought Mum some little presents. She's our mum now. All the other mums got presents too. They will all smell nice now.

We went out for walks and one day there was white stuff on the ground that came down from the sky. We thought that it was something to eat, so we tried to bury it for later, but it disappeared.

30 MARCH TO 2 APRIL 2018

Easter. I don't know what it means, but there are lots of chocolate egg things everywhere. Must keep an eye on Joey. He's already crying with excitement.

At Aunty Angela's there's lots of scrummy food for the humans – as usual. Then they all started playing a game. There was human growling and barking going on. Why can't they just play throw and bring back the ball like us?

20 APRIL 2018

Mum's got her case out again and she's driven off in Nanny Bernie's car. Oh well, Dad will be home soon and Nanny Ann won't desert us.

Dinky looking out of the window, February 2018.

Dinky and Tinsel, February 2018.

Mum comes back home in a few days and gives us lots of cuddles.

MAY 2018

Big birthday do at Aunty Debbie's. No Frankie, RIDP (rest in dog peace). It's for Aunty Debbie and Nanny Bernie. Lots of yummy food and cakes. The humans never stop eating!

Then they light the candles on the cake, sing a silly song and blow the candles out!

7 JUNE 2018

We're all going to stay at Granddad's. His human kennel is quite small, but very cosy. Everyone is going to Aunty Angela's for MORE FOOD. Us? We just get the normal boring stuff.

8 JUNE 2018

Back home now. Nanny Bernie is coming and Ashley and Sophie and the lovely little humans are coming round. Dad is cooking in the garden. Joey and me are on the lookout for sausages and burgers.

30 JUNE 2018

We're going camping! Aunty Angela and Uncle Mark arrive and leave Joseph with us. Joseph is our human cousin. Lots of little humans to play with. Mum's friend has come with her little humans and their dogs. The dogs are friendly, but behave too well, so Joey and me make our own fun by being naughty!

JULY 2018

It has been so hot again. We go for early morning walks and swims in the water.

AUGUST 2018

Mum and Nanny Bernie are off on their travels again.

15 SEPTEMBER 2018

Me, Mum and Joey are off to stay at Nanny Bernie's and John's. Great fun, lots of walks and attention!

John has lots of nice ladies come in who help him get in and out of bed! They like us – they think we are sweet and cute. Little do they know!

Mum is helping Nanny Bernie in the garden. Mum is tidying up a tree with a nasty-looking pair of giant scissors. Me and Joey are keeping out of the way. We ignore the sheep in Nanny Bernie's garden. They are not real! I went to say hello once and got a nasty bang on my head.

John has lots of nice ladies that come and help him.

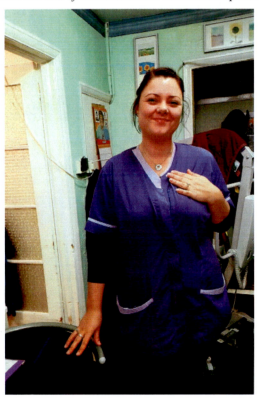

Nanny B's sheep (not real ones) in her garden, August 2018.

28 SEPTEMBER 2018

Mum AND Dad's cases are out. Serious abandonment! No – ours are out too. We're going to stay with Aunty Angela, Uncle Mark and Joseph. Never stayed there before. This could be fun! Before we go to Aunty Angela's we call in at Aunty Debbie's and Uncle Dennis's house. Dad is putting lights in their kitchen ceiling.

While he's doing this Mum takes us to Oaks Park for a walk. It's lovely there. We used to come here with Frankie.

Suddenly we saw two little pugs. It's Tinsel and Dinky from Nanny Bernie's human groomer's with their mum. We had good fun chasing each other around.

Aunty Angela and Nanny B with me and Joey in Oaks Park, September 2018.

Looking for Mum and Dad to come home, 2018.

Me and Joey staying at Aunty Angela's, September 2018.

29 SEPTEMBER 2018

Julie (John's daughter) is staying at Nanny Bernie's and John's. Julie lives in Italy.

    She had a lovely rescue dog called Cha. She adopted him from the rescue centre where she was a volunteer. Cha was our second cousin twice removed. Sadly he went to doggy heaven. How sad! RIDP.

7 OCTOBER 2018

Mum and Dad collected us from Aunty Angela's. We've had lots of fun and tried not to be too naughty! Back at home Nanny Ann has missed us all, so she says.

Dad starts his new job soon. It is much nearer and he will be here more of the time.

We will have so many humans to annoy. It's going to be a challenge – but fun!

20 OCTOBER 2018

Going to see Granddad. We went out for a walk and suddenly met two large striped animals. Mum said that they were zebras. I thought that we were in Surrey, not Africa. Mum said they weren't real, but me and Joey didn't get too close just in case.

Out walking at Granddad's we saw a (not real) zebra, October 2018.

27 OCTOBER 2018

We all went to stay at Nanny Bernie's. Nice weather, so Mum helped Nanny in the garden. The sheep have disappeared. They are in Nanny's shed. Good!

31 OCTOBER 2018

Back at home. It's Halloween. There's a funny-looking big orange ball in our kitchen window. It has a cut-out face with a candle inside and looks quite spooky.

Children come to our front door and Mum gives them sweets or money. Perhaps me and Joey could try doing it – we might get a tasty sausage or a burger!

5 NOVEMBER 2018

It's Bonfire Night or Guy Fawkes Night to humans. Lots of loud bangs and flashes. Because we are dogs we're supposed to not like the loud noises, but it doesn't bother Joey or me – we're used to it all!

DECEMBER 2018

Mum has gone mad. We think it's because it's going to be Christmas in a few weeks. Mum loves this time of year and likes to really have a good time with her family. Soon the house will be adorned with lights everywhere. The tree will appear, covered in all sorts of festive things, including chocolate stuff – must keep an eye on Joey.

Perhaps the knicker-less fairy will have been given something to put on under her dress. We hope so. It's not nice for us delicate-natured boys to see such things.

25 DECEMBER 2018

All that's left is to wish all our human and doggy friends a happy Christmas – Mum, Dad, Nanny Ann, Ashley, Sophie, little Beau and Bonnie, Nanny Bernie, John and Julie, Aunty Angela, Uncle Mark and Joseph, Aunty Debbie, Uncle Dennis, Emma and Alex, James and Sophie, Granddad and all our other human friends. Also our doggy friends – Tinsel and Dinky and others we see when out walking. And not forgetting those in doggy heaven – Holly, Frankie, Bouncer and Cha.

(Bouncer was a lovely black Labrador who belonged to Aunty Debbie and Uncle Dennis; he lived to a ripe old dog age before he went to doggy heaven. RIDP Frankie.)

Every year Nanny Bernie buys Mum a kind of book that she hangs on the wall and she writes things on the part that has got numbers on it. The other part has beautiful pictures of Bichons on it which Joey and me don't resemble at all. Mum says that it's because we are cross-bred. I've never heard of angry bread, only sliced, unsliced, brown or white. Anyway, although the dogs look very nice they don't look like they have much fun – not like Joey and me.

TUESDAY 1 JANUARY 2019

It's NEW YEAR'S DAY! Not Eve's New Ears Day!

Joey told me I was silly. He said that there isn't anyone named Eve who gets new ears every year. It's the first day of a New Year. Well, I liked Eve's New Ears Day – it was funny.

Joey can be so dogmatic sometimes. He thinks he's so clever. He keeps singing, "Oh, Micky, you're so silly."

Mum sings this to me sometimes with different words: "Oh, Micky, you're so fine."

I'll get him back soon.

Mum and Dad look really tired today. I think they went out last night to celebrate the New Year. They took me and Joey for a long walk this morning. Actually I think we took them for a walk.

WEDNESDAY 2 JANUARY 2019

Out early for a good walk. Still no sign of our sheep friends.

Mum and Dad are not working today, so we've all had a nice, cosy, cuddly day.

Mum has been writing things on the kind of book hanging on the wall. I think it's all the humans' birthdays. I hope mine and Joey's are on it. The picture for January is of a pure-white big-haired dog. I think it's a Bichon Frise, which Joey and me are supposed to be, but we don't look anything like it. Perhaps it's a throw-up, or do I mean a throwback? Anyway, Mum loves us whatever we look like – usually muddy and wet from playing in the little river.

I got my revenge on Joey today for singing that song. He was fast asleep on the chair, so I crept over and bit his tail! Mum caught me and I got told off and I'm not allowed any treats for a week. It's so unfair.

THURSDAY 3 JANUARY 2019

Very cold today, but we went for a long walk and now we're home. Mum and Dad gave us a lovely warm bath to get rid of the mud!

Oh, hello – suitcases out! Are we being abandoned again? No – our bags are out too. I wonder where we're all going?

Joey and me are going to stay at Aunty Angela's. We don't mind where we're going now. Aunty Angela, Uncle Mark and Cousin Joseph always make a fuss of us.

Mum and Dad are going to pick up Nanny Bernie tomorrow. Nanny Ann's not going; Aunty Debbie is going instead. They're all going to stay by the seaside.

FRIDAY 4 JANUARY 2019

Very cold again. We've had a good walk and now we're off!

We arrive at Aunty Angela's. I think she's pleased to see us. Then Mum and Dad go to collect Nanny Bernie.

We're going to have such a lovely time here being made a fuss of. Lots of walks and nice cuddles.

Uncle Mark likes stretching out on the settee and having a sleep, so me and Joey join him. Mum gives us Weetabix and milk for breakfast cos it's good for us. It makes Aunty Angela feel ill, so Joseph or Uncle Mark feeds us. We don't care who feeds us as long as we get fed.

SATURDAY 5 AND SUNDAY 6 JANUARY 2019

We've had a lovely time here with Aunty Angela, Uncle Mark and Cousin Joseph. Mum and Dad will be coming to collect us tomorrow.

Although we've had a good time, we will sulk when they arrive cos that's what us dogs do!

Uncle Mark, Joey and me, having a well-earned rest at Aunty Angela's, January 2019.

MONDAY 7 JANUARY 2019

Uncle Mark has given us our breakfast and we're waiting for Mum and Dad to collect us. We've had a splendid time, but there's no place like home.

They're here and making a fuss of us, but we must sulk a bit longer. Then they'll make a bigger fuss of us!

Where's Nanny Bernie? Has she been misbehaving and they've left her behind?

No – they took her home first.

Joey has got to go to the dog doctor. He's got a lump on his neck. We're all a bit worried. I wish I hadn't bit his tail now.

Joey's back from the dog doctor's. He wouldn't let the dog doctor examine him, so Mum's got to take him back tomorrow. He's very quiet. I hope he's going to be OK.

TUESDAY 8 JANUARY 2019

It's Mum's birthday. Oh crikey! I don't think we've got her a present. Dad usually gets her something from us. We'll find out later.

Mum has collected Joey from the dog doctor's. He's got infected nodules! Don't know where they are, but I'll check him out later when we go for a walk. Took a close look at Joey's nodules – they look fine to me. Not sure I'm looking in the right place, but he seems OK.

Mum's opening her presents and she gave me and Joey a big hug.

Everyone's eating cake – except us, of course. Cousin Ashley arrived with little Bonnie and Beau, Bonnie is holding something in her arms and it's moving. Me and Joey are a bit scared. It's very tiny and looks like a giant mouse. Mum said it's a chihuahua. Whatever it is we don't like it very much, but Mum says we will make friends with it soon! I don't think so. It's name is also Bonnie. Very confusing!

Mum is showing Cousin Ashley some pictures of a lovely little human baby. His name is Leo Heywood King. It sounds very posh. We've never had anyone posh in the family. Perhaps he'll be famous. He belongs to Cousin James and Sophie. We can't wait to meet him – someone else to play with.

WEDNESDAY 9 JANUARY 2019

Mum and Dad aren't working today, so we've had a lovely long sleep.

Out for walks. No sheep, but loads of muddy water in the stream.

A good warm bath when we get home! Very cosy.

Mum took us out for a short walk tonight. It's very cold and dark, but Mum says we need the exercise!

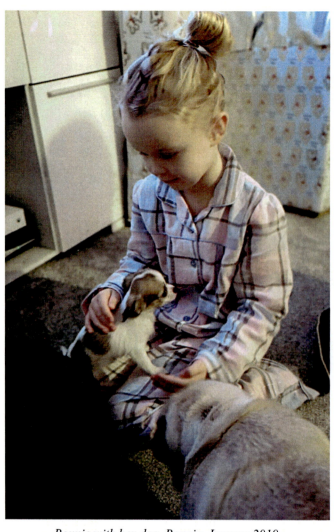

Bonnie with her dog, Bonnie, January 2019.

Leo Heywood King, January 2019.

THURSDAY 10 JANUARY 2019

Mum and Dad are not working again today. Hope they've got enough money to feed us.

My turn to be naughty today instead of Joey. Nanny Ann left her cup of coffee on the side table. I love coffee. So I crept over, climbed upon the little table, then had a good slurp. Delicious! Mum caught me and she took a photo. I suppose it's for evidence! She told me off and put me out in the garden. I will stare through the patio doors and try to look very sorry for myself, abandoned in the cold.

Oh my! Nanny Ann has come back into the room and is drinking her coffee! Mum didn't have time to say to her that I'd been drinking it, so she didn't tell her. Mum looks like she's trying not to giggle. We will have to keep a check on Nanny Ann in case she starts woofing or cocking her leg up against the furniture!

Me slurping Nanny Ann's coffee, January 2019.

FRIDAY 11 JANUARY 2019

Mum and Dad are not working again today. We're still getting fed though, so that's OK. Joey is back to normal, making a lot of noise and being a pain.

No sign of woofing or leg cocking from Nanny Ann, so she seems all right too.

Still very cold and dark, but we still go out for walks.

SATURDAY 12 JANUARY 2019

Another cold day. Still very cosy at home. Food and walks – the most important things in a dog's life!

SUNDAY 13 JANUARY 2019

Not much going on here, but me and Joey don't mind. As long as we have walks, food and cuddles we're fine.

Mum took Nanny Ann shopping. Nanny Ann didn't get us any treats. Now I won't feel bad when I slurp her coffee!

MONDAY 14 TO WEDNESDAY 16 JANUARY 2019

At last Mum and Dad are working. We were worried about getting fed!

More walks in the dark in the morning and evening.

I told Joey about the coffee incident and that we must keep a check on Nanny Ann. He just looked at me and started singing, "Oh, Micky, you're so silly."

I'll get him back soon. Must be careful though – last time I did that I bit his tail and got told off and then he wasn't very well.

THURSDAY 17 AND FRIDAY 18 JANUARY 2019

Mum doesn't usually work on Thursday and Friday so she meets Bonnie and Beau from school. It's great fun. They have their tea with us and then we play. Then Cousin Ashley picks them up. We have games with him too.

SATURDAY 19 JANUARY 2019

Mum worked on Saturday so we only had a short walk with Dad in the morning.

MONDAY 21 TO WEDNESDAY 23 JANUARY 2019

Joey is not at all well. Mum took him to the dog doctor's.
   Nothing else to write in my diary. It's so cold and dark. When will that round yellow thing in the sky warm us up again? Me and Joey have got dog depression due to lack of warm sunshine!

THURSDAY 24 AND FRIDAY 25 JANUARY 2019

Bonnie and Beau came here after school. Great fun!
   I wonder at what age me and Joey will have to go to dog school? Mum took us to puppy training a few times, but we had too much fun. So I don't think it did any good.

SATURDAY 26 AND SUNDAY 27 JANUARY 2019

Same old, same old. No warm yellow round thing in the sky. Very cosy indoors though. Lots of cosy cuddles and nice and warm.
   Joey is very ill, so Mum took him to the dog doctor's again.

He hasn't eaten anything for ages. Mum and Dad feed him baby food.

No incidents of Nanny Ann woofing or leg cocking, so I think we can presume that the case is closed!

MONDAY 28 TO THURSDAY 31 JANUARY 2019

No birthday party for me. Joey isn't at all well – he doesn't want to play or be naughty! We're all worried about him.

FRIDAY 1 FEBRUARY 2019

Joey's birthday. He had to have an operation to find out what's wrong with him.

SATURDAY 2 TO THURSDAY 7 FEBRUARY 2019

Joey went back to the dog doctor. Mum and Dad have tablets to give him, so they put them in the baby food. Dad gives him water on a spoon.

FRIDAY 8 FEBRUARY 2019

Nanny Bernie is here. Her and mum keep crying. I think it's about Joey.

SATURDAY 9 FEBRUARY 2019

Mum and Dad took Joey to the dog doctor. They came back without him. He's gone to doggy heaven!

Poor Joey. . . .

IN MEMORY OF MY LITTLE BROTHER, JOEY, RIDP
XXXXXXXXXXX

Joey.

Dogs no longer with us.

Cha, second cousin twice removed, in Italy.

Bouncer RIDP.

Holly RIDP.

Frankie RIDP.